The Art of Self-Confidence

How to Be Assertive in Any Situation

Disclaimer

No part of this Book can be transmitted or reproduced in any form including print, electronic, photocopying, scanning, mechanical or recording without prior written permission from the author.

All information, ideas and guidelines presented here are for educational purposes only. While the author has taken utmost efforts to ensure the accuracy of the written content, all readers are advised to follow information mentioned herein at their own risk. The author cannot be held responsible for any personal or commercial damage caused by misinterpretation of information. All readers are encouraged to seek professional advice when needed.

Table of Contents

Introduction

Self-confidence is nothing more than that deep-down feeling that you're basically a good person, deserving of what you have in life and of what is rightfully yours to earn. In a nutshell, self-confidence radiates power and health. Others want to be around you and to be like you. Fortunately, you can increase your self-confidence.

The self-confident are those who walk into a job interview knowing that they have the skills and knowledge to handle the position being offered. Self-confidence is embodied by the woman who asks to be promoted based on her assurance that, because of her previous efforts, she deserves the promotion. The chapters in this book all focus on helping you become someone who is naturally and easily influential to others, more visible, and yes, even more attractive, without getting cosmetic surgery.

Everywhere you look, there are lifelong career professionals losing confidence in their ability to stay competitive in a rapidly changing society. At the same time, no one in society has a long-term lock on any market niche, and no body of information affords a strategic competitive advantage for long. The reality of our times is that everyone is feeling at least a little unsure of himself, and in that sense everyone is in the same boat.

One of the secrets about radiant, self-confident people is that they know where they shine and where they don't. Either through logical analysis or intuition, they have determined when and where they are at their best and how to be at their best more of the time.

One prominent psychologist likened self-doubt to a living death. He said it could consume so much of your energy and exuberance that you spend unending hours seeking to correct whatever supposedly isn't working in your life. You then engage in self-management and self-improvement campaigns and are nearly left apart from yourself, constantly battling your innermost thoughts and emotions, striving for some unattainable notion of perfection.

So, in this book, well explore the ever-vital concept of self-confidence. Whatever level of self-confidence you currently maintain, I promise that even greater potential awaits.

1. Vocal Self-Confidence

In this chapter, I'm going to discuss how to increase your vocal self-confidence, offering strategies you can adopt and steps you can take to learn and practice conveying to others through your voice that you're in command.

There are people in my life, and undoubtedly in yours, who, when they say something, prompt you to act. It's something in the way they speak—their measured tones, often speaking in a deeper bass voice, but not necessarily so —that summons something within me to take notice.

If you've never regarded your voice as a tool for being more confident and self-confident in this life, you're in for some revelations. I'm not going to ask you to change your voice. (Unless you have already repeatedly received feedback to the contrary, chances are, you don't need to make it lower or higher.)

By practicing what you learn in this chapter, you'll make the best of the voice God gave you. As with all change, you can't expect a miracle overnight. It's about setting some reasonable expectations for yourself. Although not everything presented here may be your cup of tea, by following most of what's recommended one step at a time, you'll rack up small achievements that spur you on to even greater confidence.

You don't develop real-world self-confidence in cyberspace, and you don't develop vocal self-confidence using a keyboard. People who have vocal self-confidence quite naturally are out there speaking in front of others. Happily, you have opportunities to do this all day long, day in and day out.

Do you realize that every half hour you speak to someone, you're producing an amount of text equivalent to 20 transcribed pages? If you were to take such transcription, clean it up, and eliminate the redundancies, you'd end up with about 14 to 16 pages of material.

In other words, for every two minutes that you're speaking to someone, you are creating the equivalent of one complete manuscript page. So, there can be no more discussion about a lack of opportunity to get in some practice.

To understand who has vocal self-confidence, you need to pay attention to people who talk to you. Let's start with those who apparently do not have it. These are people who:

- Don't speak in clear, resonant tones.

- Stumble over their words.

- Use sentences punctuated by "um," "er," and "ah."

- Inject "you know," "it's like," and other verbal asides that only distract from a listener's ability to gain meaning.

Effective speaking increasingly is becoming a highly demanded attribute of rising career professionals. Nearly every organization wants technologically competent professionals who can reasonably articulate their thoughts.

I'm not saying you have to become an orator of the same caliber as William Jennings Bryan, develop the elocution skills of Winston Churchill, or make deliveries with the drama and emotion of Jesse Jackson; far from it. Indeed, some of the most persuasive people you may know, those who have oodles of vocal self-confidence, maybe relatively unskilled as public speakers.

On a one-to-one basis, in a small group setting, or, when the situation merits, in a larger group setting, some people are able to convey their thoughts and ideas, wishes or demands to others so that everyone in the room understands the first time. Those with vocal self-confidence don't necessarily have the best grammar or diction, but it helps.

Some people, by virtue of their size or physical appearance, well-developed muscles, or other distinguishing physical characteristics, seem naturally to catch the attention of others. Most of the rest of us have to work a little more on it.

While there are all kinds of techniques you can use to strengthen your voice and improve your delivery, in the end, the fastest and easiest wav to become more vocally self-confident is simply to practice speaking to others in a more confident way. You wanted to hear that, didn't you? I mean, it's a lot easier than having to undergo hours of instruction!

There are simple techniques you can practice right now, especially if no one else is nearby, to give your vocal cords a good workout.

When you get up in the morning, do you practice using your voice just as you'd practice using any of your other muscles? Probably not. I suggest running through the vowels in a harmonic way. Say out loud, Aaaaay, Eeeee, Iiiii, Ooooo, Uuuuu. Then, do it almost as if you're singing them.

Next, try some long words. Out loud, say:

- Discombobulate

- Prestidigitation

- Clavicle

- Philanthropical

- Aphrodisiac

When you've said those a couple times, try some geography:

- Monongahela River

- Mount Kilimanjaro

- Tahiti

- The Susquehanna River

- The Tigris and the Euphrates

- The Mekons Delta

By giving yourself a vocal workout you'll be potentially more expressive all day.

Have a warm drink early in the morning. Your vocal chords will thank you. Cold drinks contract the vocal chords, making it harder for you to use them.

If you have a sore or weak voice or throat, try holding your jaw with your hands. Put one hand under each side of your jaw so that your fingers touch your ears and your palms are under your chin. This brings immediate warmth to the area and helps to loosen you up.

Also, yawn frequently, especially if you're alone where you can let out a big, loud yawn. Lions yawn all the time, and you don't see anyone ignoring their roar.

It also helps to rotate your shoulders around and around in one direction, then in the alternate direction. Stretches, particularly those where your arms are above your head, can also help.

Orchestra conductors live longer than the average person. Perhaps it's because they keep their hands above their heart; that is, their circulatory systems are strengthened while they work.

Breathing plays an important role in your ability to convey authority in your voice. Don't be afraid to talk breathily on occasion, but don't make it your standard mode of delivery. Sigh when you need to and even hum. The following exercises all help to unlock energy:

• Make gentle out-breaths.

• Hold your breath for a moment, and then suddenly release it.

• Yell. (This one works best when you're alone.)

What part do your lungs play in establishing vocal authority? Strong lungs help achieve more effective breathing. If you're born with strong lungs, thank your lucky stars.

The only thing you can do to potentially improve your lung capacity' is swim. Researchers think that this is because of the increased pressure on your lungs when you are in the water. The way to make your lungs weaker is clear: Exercise in polluted air near carbon monoxide, or in cities where the smog level is high. Also smoke heavily until regular wheezing and coughing become natural for you.

You have probably heard this before, but it warrants repeating because it's so true, and so few people pay any homage to it. The most effective and efficient breathing is done by using the abdominal muscles rather than the rib cage. Whenever you use your diaphragm (located on the inside of your stomach roughly where your navel is) to do the work instead of your rib muscles, you're far more efficient.

The fastest way to understand diaphragmatic breathing is to lie down on the floor, place your hands over your midsection, and breathe normally. Do you feel your stomach going up and down? That's diaphragmatic breathing, and you can do it while you're standing or sitting.

If you've been speaking for a while and you notice that your breathing is shallow, try to bounce a little. Let your knees unlock and go up and down just an inch or so. A mild bounce actually helps you engage your diaphragm while you breathe. Hence, you breathe more efficiently, and are able to summon your resources and maintain vocal strength.

Clavicular-shoulder breathing is evident when you raise and lower your collarbones and shoulders as you inhale and exhale. This is an inefficient way to breathe.

Too many highly athletic types make the mistake of raising their shoulders as well as expanding their rib cages to draw a strong, deep breath. During the heat of battle, such as when you have been racing up and down a basketball court, it makes perfect sense to breathe this way. In fact, you probably have little choice. At a resting pulse rate, athletes would be better off breathing using the diaphragm only.

Sit-ups and crunches are helpful for abdominal conditioning, but you also need to give these muscles aerobic conditioning on a regular basis. What is the single best aerobic exercise? Walking.

Have you ever received a phone call from someone you haven't heard from in years? Even though he or she didn't announce who it was for a few moments, you knew instantly, and you only needed to hear a word or two. Perhaps they only said hello and your name.

Like your fingerprints, your voice is unique. Yes, some people sound quite a bit like others, just like some fingerprints are close to others, but they are all different.

Your voice has a "music" to it. This is defined by how loudly or softly you speak, how quickly or slowly you speak, whether your pitch rises or falls at the end of sentences, and other characteristics such as richness, texture, and timbre.

What about lower tones? What you may have heard is true. Those who use the lower end of their voice range tend to appear more self-confident. Why?

• Low pitch equates to being in control of your emotions and the situation you face.

• High pitch conveys excitement and possibly fear, insecurity, or nervousness.

Experts say that vocal variety is the key to being an interesting conversationalist and someone to whom others will pay attention. If you want to convey high energy, you can actually tone down your pitch a notch or two. Contrary to Hollywood movies and most TV sitcoms, loud booming voices and ranting and raving behavior grate on your listeners' nerves after a while.

Following are some quick but effective tips for improving your speech:

- Use vocal variety for a more interesting presentation.

- To convey more energy, tone down your pitch a notch.

- Use broad sweeping gestures and a booming voice in moderation. These begin to wear on the audience.

- Tape yourself while practicing your presentation. Then play it back and critique yourself.

- Eliminate "um," "uh," and "er." They add nothing to your communications.

- When you need vocal strength, a mild bounce right where you're standing will summon your resources.

- Keep your jaw relaxed as you speak.

The proof is in the pudding, or, if you're a Fried Green Tomatoes fan, the secret is in the sauce. You'll know you've achieved a notable level of vocal self-confidence when you get in front of others and they:

1. Tell you that you're a new and improved you.

2. Do what you say with a lot less resistance.

Now, let's cover a few fundamentals of how to be more effective every time you open your mouth.

It's Not What Is Said, It's How It's Said

Any audience you're speaking to, whether it's a party of one or one thousand, assesses you on many different levels, not only on what you say, but how you say it. Hence, you want to open your part of the conversation or presentation with authority. Communicate with your eyes that you're in control.

Let your audience know that you're speaking to them, not to your notes, the back of the room, the microphone, or the ceiling. Try to be as relaxed and comfortable as you can in front of any group. The vocally self-confident have the magical ability to be themselves, whether speaking with one or many. They know that there's no need to change.

Certainly, in front of a large group, any gestures you use need to be larger. The pauses between your sentences need to be a tad longer. Convey your message with your eyes, mouth, body, and heart. To be at your influential best, stand erect with your best posture. A stiff body, clenched fist, or unanimated expression makes it tough for your listeners to be on your side as they follow along with you.

Appeal to your audience's emotions and intellect, but primarily to their emotions. If you're not naturally animated, work on your facial expressions, gestures, and movement about the podium. If you are naturally animated, thank your lucky stars, but keep trying to improve on how you use your speaking gift.

Start with small groups, perhaps speaking to a neighbor, co-worker, staff member, or even a spouse. On each occasion, try to master one new element of advancing your vocal authority. The first time, perhaps, fully pronounce the "ing" at the end of words.

Another time, work on becoming comfortable with pausing between sentences, and, perhaps another time, use some dramatic hand gestures that are outside of your normal repertoire. No one is likely to know what you're doing, but they may begin to notice the difference in your effectiveness.

Advanced Exercises

Here are some advanced exercises to improve your speech:

- To improve your diction, practice speaking with marbles in your mouth, or with a pencil sideways. Also practice intentionally over-enunciating.

- Use exercises to elongate your speaking channel. For example, stick your tongue all the way out, all the way up, left, right, on your back molars as if you're trying to swallow peanut butter, and roll forward.

- Try tongue-twisters to get good at handling lots of words. You know, the old "Peter Piper picked a peck of pickled peppers."

- Practice speaking while dribbling a basketball or engaging in some other physical activity.

- Practice speaking loudly and softly.

- Practice giving certain words emphasis.

So...

- Vocal self-confidence tells others that you are confident and in control.

- To improve your level of vocal self-confidence, practice in front of the mirror, with the camcorder rolling, or with an audiocassette recorder.

- You can strengthen your vocal chords much as you can strengthen muscles in your body. Practice saying long words, melodious words, vowel sounds, and consonant combinations such as "st," "ch," "sp," and "sh."

- Practice in front of real-life subjects as well, starting with one-on-one situations and small groups.

- Find a speech pattern you can live with and which is influential to others, and you can stay with it for a lifetime.

2. Basic Self-Confidence Tips

Let's jump right into some specific strategies you can use to build your self-confidence unfailingly, naturally, and easily.

Rome wasn't built in a day. You've heard that before? How about this: The Chicago Bulls didn't win a championship in the first six seasons that Michael Jordan played with them. Happily, it won't take you seven years to develop more self-confidence. You actually can see results in as little as seven days, even more in 21 days, and magnificent results within a few months.

Suppose you're a salesperson and have a territory that you cover by car. How much better would each of your presentations be if you spent a few minutes in the car carefully collecting your thoughts, perhaps reviewing or rearranging your notes, taking a few deep breaths, and contemplating how you would like the encounter to unfold? Do you realize that many of the world's top income earners, even years into professional selling, still spend significant amounts of time preparing before each sales call? In many respects, what these top producers are doing is simply going over the basics. They know that preparation, even a few minutes worth, is worth its weight in gold in terms of boosting self-confidence.

The basics are what propel top performers all over the world. Olympic athletes, major league baseball players, chess masters, you name it. All spend time at the beginning of each season or each contest reviewing the fundamentals. It's the mediocre performers who think they can skip vital steps. They get bored, or they assume that they're naturally doing everything okay.

While practice doesn't always make perfect, practice does help you increase performance in every endeavor.

You may have noticed that self-confident people seem to resonate an inner calm. Even in a crisis situation, they appear to have a sense of equanimity that impacts every aspect of their lives.

The best athletes play with fire and intensity, while maintaining an air of relaxation. By staying focused and relaxed, you can empty your mind of distractions and, hence, increase your ability to perform, regardless of the task at hand.

Equanimity is the ability to maintain balance and perspective, even in the face of turmoil.

Extending yourself for the express purpose of impressing others runs counter to the notion of self-confidence. You end up spending more time and energy doing things simply because you want to impress others.

In the grand mix of activities in which you engage in life, there's certainly nothing wrong with doing things to please or occasionally impress others. The issue is, do you have a choice?

The self-confident person engages in such activities, or does not, at will. He recognizes that he's most likely to succeed at those things that he enjoys doing, and as the situation dictates, he looks for ways to include others.

Trust Others

Few individuals make it in society without the help and support of others. Even if you're an entrepreneur, there are frequent times throughout the day and week when you need to rely on others. The self-confident person in a work setting delegates freely and easily, but also carefully and methodically. He or she knows that the confidence placed in others helps create a victorious circle, wherein both parties bolster each others confidence.

Perhaps the saddest, most pitiful people you're likely to know are those who cannot place trust in others. They vehemently cling to whatever projects, information, or good fortune may come their way. They neither share nor benefit from the synergy that could occur from letting others into their "private" domain.

The great leaders of the world, some of the most self-confident people among us, are able to engender a loyal following because they trust people. The greater the trust, the greater the following.

If you win small victories all day long and acknowledge them as such, your subconscious will begin to believe that you are indeed a winner. After all, you rack up victories every day.

Before you discount this as some type of self-congratulatory system, consider that since the subconscious makes no assessment about the magnitude of your victories but earnestly works to support you in garnering more of the same, each time you acknowledge yourself, whether the accomplishment is large or small, you set in motion the internal apparatus that will increase the probability of you achieving even more.

Reward Yourself

When you do something wonderful, take time out of your day to not only acknowledge yourself, but to do something nice for yourself. Stop off and get an ice-cream cone. Go to that movie you want to see.

Self-confident people understand the vital importance of enjoying their successes.

If you treat each day and each event as just part of the job or one of many responsibilities, all days begin to look the same. What are some good activities and events for which you can have at least a mini-celebration? The list is very long. Try these for openers. When you:

- Complete a report prior to the deadline

- Are under budget this quarter

- Finish three strokes under your handicap

- Complete your taxes

- Clean out and organize your garage

- Drop those six pounds you've been seeking to shed

- Finally decide to book that vacation in Martinique

Mistakes

All, if life were nothing but victories! Everyone makes mistakes by the boatload, but confident people somehow learn along the way that mistakes need not drag them down. They don't dwell on them. They regard them as life lessons that give them insights that perhaps they did not have before.

Cut yourself some slack. Give yourself some leeway to make mistakes on occasion and be far less than perfect, especially when it comes to being self-confident.

Life repeats itself until you learn the lesson, and then you move on. If you were to never make any mistakes or make only tiny ones, that would be a sign that you probably weren't attempting enough in life. After all, if you play it safe, hardly taking your foot off first base, you'll never get picked off, but you won't score many runs either.

Conjure up the image of someone you know who is self-confident. Does she go to pieces when she makes a mistake? Does she get bogged down in what didn't go right, or does she learn from it and move on?

Going a Step Beyond

Self-confident people are not afraid to use their imaginations. They've come to draw upon imagination as a creative, visual, internal rehearsal of what can be. Consider this—how often does stuff just fall into your lap? How often does good fortune smile on you, when you've had no hand in it at all? I'm guessing far less than you'd like it to happen.

Conversely, how often do things work out for the best, when you at least contemplated the possibilities? A bit more often, I'll wager. Those who lack confidence are afraid to engage their imagination, as if there will be some kind of penalty for having the temerity to wish for more.

A philosopher once said, "The imagination is the workshop of the mind." Visualization is one of the many tools of imagination. Here are some ideas to imagine your way to greater self-confidence:

- Imagine yourself giving an effective presentation to your team on Wednesday.

- Imagine yourself going up to someone you're attracted to and easily initiating a conversation.

- Imagine marching into your boss's office and, in a relaxed and confident manner, discussing why it's time for you to receive a raise.

- Imagine the press eagerly writing down what you have to say.

- Imagine being self-confident whenever you choose to be.

If you could arrange your life so that you were surrounded by self-confident people, human nature being what it is, eventually you'd become more like them. Unfortunately, it's not likely you can structure your life to be around self-confident people all the time. You have got to interact with people from all parts of the behavioral spectrum. Hereafter, though, if you remain cognizant of who's self-confident and the distinctions between his or her behavior and that of others, you may just be among the lucky few who awake one bright morning and find that they, too, are highly self-confident people.

So...

- Practice nearly every day the many simple strategies for increasing your self-confidence.

- Prepare, prepare, prepare. The most accomplished among us keep returning to the basics.

- Look for the small victories as well as the large in everything you do, and reward yourself often.

- Don't dwell on your mistakes, but learn from them and then move on.

- Use your imagination to devise scenarios in which you act in ways that you normally don't allow yourself.

- Hang around, observe, and imitate self-confident people. Self-confidence leaves clues.

3. Wealth and Self-Esteem

If you're the eldest child in your family, supposedly you are inclined to be more self-confident. True sometimes, but not across the board. I've even heard it said that if you are from an affluent family you tend to be more self-confident than someone from less well-to-do origins.

Let's take a brief tour to see if these notions hold water.

From Little Orphan Annie to Richie Rich, an age-old question persists: What advantages are there to being raised in an affluent environment? More specifically, is there a link between wealth and self-esteem? Are the wealthy wealthy because they're self-confident? Does someone raised in affluence tend to become self-confident?

It appears that self-esteem does indeed lead to wealth. Denis Waitely, who from the early 1970s to the early 1990s studied wealthy, successful, high achievers from all walks of life, found a strong correlation between a strong vocabulary and greater income-producing potential. This doesn't mean that merely having an extensive vocabulary or being verbose adds up to self-esteem or wealth. Brilliant Ph.D.s may speak poetically on one topic and give an extended philosophical discourse on another, but may not be self-confident. Perhaps you had a professor in college like that. Perhaps you are a professor like that. A good vocabulary, however, certainly helps.

The natural ability to speak up is a valuable skill. In addition, the self-confident tend to rise faster in their careers and, yes, earn more money.

Within professional service firms, the "finders," people who go out and get new business, earn much more than the "minders" who manage the projects, and the "grinders" who actually do the work. In large organizations, the people who make themselves heard rise to the top.

Some of the very wealthy asserted themselves at a young age. Whatever else you may think of him, Henry Ross Perot is an excellent example of someone from humble origins and short of stature, who, by virtue of his self-esteem, generated nearly incalculable wealth.

Perot grew up in the Depression era. At age 12, he approached the circulation manager of his town newspaper, the Gazette, and offered to deliver newspapers to people's homes in the poverty-stricken area of town. No one had ever conceived of this idea—the prevailing assumption was that poor people could not afford, let alone read, a newspaper. Perot felt otherwise.

Within a short period Perot was making so much money by delivering newspapers that his commission was in jeopardy of being reduced. Never one to sit back and let others control his destiny, Perot wrote to the publisher and complained about how he was being treated by the paper's management after making so much money for the paper. The publisher agreed with him and he was able to continue the lucrative arrangement he had set up.

While working for IBM and becoming their top sales representative, Perot conceived of initiating a service branch within IBM which would help client companies learn how to use and apply office technology to improve their business operations. IBM declined to follow through on his idea, and Perot, at age 31, decided to leave his high-commission-earning job to start his own company, EDS. In 1984, he sold EDS to General Motors for $2.5 billion, and in 1986 sold his remaining stock in the company for $700 million. In one move after another, Perot asserted himself on the way to his ultimate prosperity.

Consider Kavelle R. Bajaj, who came to the United States from India in 1974 and faced cultural and gender barriers. In her conservative Indian upbringing, Bajaj was expected to place family affairs over a career. She opened a small business selling imported goods, but almost immediately became dissatisfied and disappointed in this venture.

Eventually she opted to try again. In the early 1980s, following the breakup of American Telephone and Telegraph, Bajaj borrowed $5,000 and took computer and database management classes at a nearby college. She then started a company called I-Net, which provided telecommunication contracting services primarily to the Department of Defense.

The company developed a solid reputation and grew quickly, if not evenly, over the next several years. In 1990, Bajaj landed a $100-million long-term contract from the Air Force for computer systems engineering and software. Bajaj attributes her success to initiative, self-esteem, and commitment to ideals. "There is opportunity in the United States for the person who wants to make it," she says. "There is no reason to make excuses."

The Ways and the Means

If self-esteem leads to wealth, does wealth lead to self-esteem? Those who are wealthy have the means to make their wishes more readily known than those who are not as wealthy. If you're wealthy, perhaps you have more time to be in organizations and take leadership positions. Certainly, someone who is wealthy has more options in life than someone who is not.

Historically, men have been heads of nations, leaders of governments, generals, warriors, orators, debaters, professors, and scholars. They were more likely to be published, broadcast, and celebrated. Male children emulated their fathers, while female children emulated their mothers. Once again, however, your ability to be self-confident, whether you're a man or a woman, is dependent mostly on the unique and particular aspects of your own situation.

Everything that you've encountered in this book, including this chapter, shows that you can learn to be more self-confident, regardless of whatever potential disadvantages, impediments, or obstacles may be in your path. In fact, you can look for small victories in everyday life that will enhance your ability to be self-confident.

4. Physical Self-Esteem

In this chapter, well explore what physical self-esteem is all about and how you can project it. You don't necessarily need to run to the gym and pick up the barbells. Instead, you'll merely learn how to project that you're in control.

Physical self-esteem is the ability to convey with your body and demeanor that you can stand up for yourself and you're in charge.

If you speak to the police in your community, you'll find that they have at least a loose profile of the typical victim of a mugging. Independent of sex and age, those most prone to be attacked:

- Walk with shoulders slumped forward.

- Look down.

- Have poor posture.

- Do not swing their arms.

- Seem unaware of the larger surroundings.

Conversely, independent of sex and age, those less likely to be targets of muggings exhibit at least a few if not all of the following characteristics:

- Walk with an even stride.

- Swing their arms a little.

- Keep their heads up.

- Take in much if not all of their surroundings.

- Have good posture.

- Take the seat of your choice.

- Maintain good posture.

- Dress well.

- Prepare.

- Smile.

- Maintain a pleasant demeanor.

- Speak at an even and unhurried pace.

- Firmly shake hands.

- Take the initiative to heartily greet the other party.

- Remain in control during the meeting.

- Deliver your points with gusto.

- Leave at the appropriate time.

- Stride out with vigor.

What about those times when you were a shrinking violet, not at your best? What can you recall about the messages that you imparted, either verbal or nonverbal?

Now, think back to some time when you were more of a shrinking violet. Do you recall that you:

- Didn't look the other party right in the eye?

- Didn't speak with authority?

- Weren't confident entering the room?

- Didn't take the seat of your choice?

- Didn't maintain good posture?

- Weren't dressed well?

- Weren't well prepared?

- Didn't smile?

- Didn't maintain a pleasant demeanor?

- Didn't speak at an even and unhurried pace?

- Didn't firmly shake hands?

- Didn't take the initiative to heartily greet the other party?

- Didn't remain in control during the meeting?

- Didn't deliver your points with gusto?

- Didn't leave at the appropriate time?

- Didn't stride out with vigor?

Now, for the Illinois Lotto Jackpot, here's your question: What was the difference between the times you were your dynamic self, projecting physical self-esteem, and those when you were your shrinking-violet self, projecting wimpiness? Chances are, you felt confident in those situations in which you projected well, and experienced a lack of confidence in those situations where you came off as a dishrag.

Body language is critical in establishing a positive image.

Body language certainly accounts for a sizable chunk of the message you impart to others. The simple key to projecting an aura of greater physical self-esteem is self-awareness. When you're aware of what your body imparts to others, the changes you need to make come naturally and easily.

It's not mandatory for you to hit the gym, but you don't see many couch potatoes who are that physically self-confident. Even the mildest exercise will help you stay in reasonable physical shape and, hence, help you to project to others. If you belong to a health club or a gym, undoubtedly you know that a variety of weight machines are available today that can help you work out virtually any muscle group in your body.

Health professionals say that working out for as little as 30 minutes three times a week is sufficient to give you vim and vigor.

Free weights and various pulley machines are available in most health clubs or gyms. Many of the exercises you can do with weights help strengthen your upper body, which in turn helps your posture. When you're able to throw your chest out and your shoulders back naturally as you walk, you breathe more efficiently, stand up straighter, tire less easily, and appear more physically self-confident.

Why do some people command your respect, even when they say nothing to you or do nothing in particular? Beyond how you carry yourself, and how your body moves, many other factors contribute to your physical self-esteem. Let's review each of these briefly, keeping an eye on ways you can convey the kind of message to others that you want to.

Facial Expression

Do you go around smiling all day? Do you frown or scowl? Those facial expressions convey messages; a blank expression conveys little. If you have a blank expression on your face, no matter what you're saying, the other party will have a hard time "hearing you" and look for other clues, such as your body language and voice, to get your overall message.

The blank of face are not giving you enough of the cues you are accustomed to receiving in conversation with others. Hence, you have to pay attention even more closely to get their meaning.

If you're the person with the blank expression, this may explain why it often appears that no one is listening to you. Use your face to express meaning!

Voice Strength and Quality

Are you among the masses who ramble, mumble, or otherwise truncate words? Are you normally soft spoken, particularly when you need more vocal power to convey your message? Many people have particular problems with using their voices when it comes to meeting a stranger, speaking to others over the telephone, or speaking to a group.

If you know someone who frequently speaks to you with a blank expression, you now know why you find yourself consistently drifting off when this person speaks to you. You'll have to engage all of your listening skills to gain a fuller meaning of their message.

Posture

Regarding posture, mentally review how you go about your day. Do you sit up straight in your chair, or are you frequently slumped over? Is your chair at the proper height for you to use your desk, computer, telephone, and other equipment? When conversing with others, say, in the hallway, do you frequently lean on the wall or a table, or do you stand erect but relaxed?

Eye Contact

Whether you're speaking to someone or listening, your use of eye contact says a lot about you. Looking at someone only intermittently, looking past him, or looking down at the floor is a much less effective means of keeping him in the conversation and having him heed what you say.

Instead, maintain more extended eye contact. I'm not talking about staring somebody down, fixating on him to the point where you don't ever turn away. That can be considered rude and disconcerting, among other things. I am talking about holding your eye contact for at least three to five seconds at some points, and as long as 20 to 25 seconds at others.

You can break this up by nodding occasionally, briefly looking up at the ceiling or down at the floor when you're trying to recall something or come up with a point, pointing to a chalkboard or document between you, or simply glancing away for a moment in any direction.

Think about the times when you had a conversation with someone who avoided eye contact with you at all costs:

- Was this person influential?

- Did their words have the most impact possible?

- Did you feel comfortable about the conversation?

Chances are, you answered no in all three cases. Others may feel the same if they are in conversation with you and your eves are everywhere except on them.

Use of Gestures

Gestures help those around you more fully understand what you're trying to convey.

If you're like most people, you're probably unaware of the gestures you use when speaking to others. Some gestures help you make your point and win the attention and respect of others.

Other gestures, including those you probably impart unconsciously, can actually detract from your message and say, "I don't really intend to follow up on this," or "I don't intend to hold you accountable."

A lot of misinformation about what some gestures mean has been handed down over the years. For example, dozens if not hundreds of books suggest that if someone's arms are folded across his chest, he's conveying defensiveness and appearing closed to the information being presented. This could be true on occasion, but it is largely hogwash. A person might fold his arms across his chest for a number of reasons, including the following:

- He might be cold, and crosses his arms and hands across his chest for warmth.

- He might be bored but still not defensive.

- He might simply feel comfortable with his hands in that position.

Certainly, any fidgeting, nervous tapping, or other involuntary gestures you display repeatedly may distract the other party and diminish the impact of your message. We've all been in conversation with someone who taps their foot, fidgets with a pen or pencil, or frequently scratches their ear. Most likely, these types of gestures do not add to that person's interpersonal effectiveness, but detract from it.

Moving in too close to someone can be as ineffective as pulling away from them. Many people don't like to have someone, "in their face," and may get defensive or feel threatened. This will detract from their ability to actually hear you, and they may capitulate in the short run, not adding to a climate of respect or trust.

Here are some vocal detractors, the presence of which will diminish the impact of your message, followed by the antidotes:

• Stiff or formal speech

Antidote: Spice up your language, use contractions, put down your notes.

• Gross mispronunciation of words, particularly common words

Antidote: Use a dictionary to look up words and practice enunciating them before uttering them to others.

• Overuse of cliches, slang, and hackneyed expressions

Antidote: Listen to yourself on tape and pick out overused expressions. Also ask others if you overuse some phrases.

• Use of non-sequiturs

Antidote: Stick to the main point; don't ramble.

• Overuse of filler language, such as "um," "er," "ah," "you see," and "you know"

Antidote: Give yourself more time between sentences. Get comfortable with pausing in silence between phrases or thoughts instead of relying on "um," "er."

"ah," and "you know" types of unnecessary connectors.

• Lack of clarity

Antidote: Think about the point of your message in advance. Lead to it all along.

• Failure to come to a coherent point Antidote: Have your strong point ready. Mentally rehearse it before speaking.

Vocal Self-Esteem

We all know people who are vocally self-confident but not physically self-confident. These are people who, by virtue of their positions, demand you pay attention to them. One of these people may be your boss, or some bureaucrat who speaks with authority but never gets out of his chair.

It's possible as well to have physical self-esteem without vocal self-esteem. Generally, however, the two go hand in hand. Someone who has good posture, stands tall, uses gestures appropriately, and has sufficient eye contact has the best chance of being heard, understood, and heeded.

When you can combine physical self-esteem with vocal self-esteem, also known as vocal authority, you're cooking with gas heat! It helps if you have a rich, deep, bass voice, but if you don't, take heart. Millions of people all over the planet with far less than rich, melodious voices still manage to have vocal authority. It's all a matter of how you use your voice.

You want to employ vocal variety and engage your listeners—let them know that you're speaking to them, not to your notes, the back of the room, the microphone, or the ceiling.

Over the years, much has been written about walking your talk. I'd like to introduce, for the first time in this universe, the importance of talking your walk—using your voice in a manner that connotes vocal self-esteem and is consistent with the physical self-esteem you may also display.

Walking your talk is a worn-out cliche that essentially means you personally live up to what you talk about; that is, you practice what you preach.

If you are able to talk your walk, you have the best of both worlds. Everything about you says, "When I speak, there's a good chance it's worth listening to."

So...

- Conveying physical self-esteem is based less on your size, weight, or muscles and more on how you carry and project yourself.

- You convey alertness and awareness to others mainly through your eyes.

- You don't have to exercise to convey strength or authority. However, it can't hurt, and it certainly can help.

- Effective use of gestures helps the other party stay attuned to what you're saying.

- Being both physically and vocally self-confident gets others to listen and respond to you.

5. Family Members and Self-Confidence

In his book, Care of the Soul, Thomas Moore says that human beings are "infinitely complicated and profound." He observes that our family relationships might be good or not so good, but in either case, we could understand them better if we more often acknowledged just how complicated and profound other members of our family can be. Many of our family members have a history that we'll never know; that is, a history that they've created during the time they're away from us.

Moore also suggests that instead of trying to diagnose or predict the behavior of our spouse, parents, or children, we could better spend our time appreciating them for who and what they are. That in itself undoubtedly would improve family relations.

Undoubtedly, you've experienced firsthand the rigors of attempting to be self-confident within your immediate family. Do you find yourself falling into familiar communication patterns when interacting with members of your family to try to get someone to do something or drive a point home?

Perhaps a major impediment to being self-confident within your immediate family is the sheer proximity of your family members. It's easy to fall into the mindset that you know all about them because you see them so frequently— what their views are, how they'll respond, what sets them off, and how you are set off by them.

You tell your child to straighten up his room and you notice he barely lifts a finger. You raise your voice, and he moves a little faster.

You come back in a few minutes, and perhaps he is dawdling again. You reemphasize what you want him to do. Now, however, you sound like your parents when they talked that way to you 28 years ago.

Perhaps you're having a discussion with your spouse about where you want to go on your next vacation. Your spouse says the mountains, and you say the shore. You present your case; your spouse presents his case. Neither side really listens, and the conversation degenerates into a spat.

You may realize you've been down this trail before. Once you become a little heated, the argument takes on a life of its own. The net effect is you are anything but self-confident.

A growing body of evidence suggests that to be effective with members of your immediate family, or anyone else for that matter, you need to connect with that other person so that she actually thinks you're on her side. In other words, achieving the outcome you seek often involves helping the other person achieve the outcome they seek.

There's no need to think that every interpersonal encounter you have with members of your family hereafter means you have to go out of your way to help them achieve something in a tit-for-tat manner. Sometimes the other party needs only to gain a sense of respect, attention, caring, or some other feeling that you can impart while asserting yourself.

When you engage in tit-for-tat behavior with someone, you match the magnitude and frequency of the other person's actions.

If you're like many people, you may need to let your internal engine rev down after work before interacting with your family. After all, you're not talking to Joe in accounting, Sally in marketing, Hal in logistics, or Jennifer in the Springfield division anymore.

Here's a quick quiz to help remind you that professional self-esteem is not the same as self-esteem in your family. Before making your wishes known at home...

• Have you taken three deep breaths?

• Do you exchange pleasantries?

• Do you ask your spouse or children how their day went?

• Do you make eye contact and speak face-to-face?

• Do you give your complete and undivided attention?

• Do you use polite and complimentary language?

• Do you offer praise or acknowledgment for something other family members have done?

• Have you pitched in on some household task or chore?

Here's how to score your answers. If you answered "yes" to seven or more of the above, you're probably fooling yourself. If you answered "yes" four to six times, your family will probably be responsive to you. If you answered "yes" three times or less, you need to take immediate action. Review the list again and decide which five gestures you'll employ tomorrow after work.

If you are a gung-ho, career-climbing world-beater, arriving home still mentally immersed in the affairs of the workday and revving at the pace of business, members of your family may have difficulty relating to you, let alone heeding you.

Your Spouse

Is it harder today to be in a marriage or a relationship than in previous eras? It's an issue I won't explore in detail, but undoubtedly you have some opinions about this. In an era in which divorce rates are high and some domestic quarrels make the evening news, it's safe to say that it's difficult for many spouses to interact effectively with one another these days.

Open any of a number of women's or men's magazines, and you'll find that communicating with one's partner is at the top of the list in articles on relationship problems.

Thomas Moore says that each marriage has its own identity, direction, and movement. It takes on a life beyond the original intentions of either spouse. Because the roots of any spousal interaction (including any argument) may go back to the very start of the relationship, marriages or other intimate relationships may well be the toughest relationships to keep vibrant and on an even keel.

When you know your spouse is willing to really listen to you, and vice versa, you both can be more effective at resolving differences of perspective or opinion. Besides drawing on everything you've learned up to this point, here's an extensive checklist of behaviors and communication techniques you may wish to use on your next encounter:

• Minimize any negative feelings you have before speaking.

• Eliminate the notion that your partner "should have done this" or "could have done that."

• Contemplate how he/she might view the issue you're about to discuss.

• Let go of feelings of omniscience or superiority.

• Realize that your way may be the way this time, but it's not always so.

• Look for the good in your partner.

• Consider things to appreciate rather than issues to analyze.

Once you engage in conversation, especially if there is a chance that the conversation might get heated, your challenge to remain self-confident becomes even greater. If you recall and employ even a few of the following interpersonal communication techniques, you're bound to have more favorable results:

Start your sentences with the following phrases

61

"I would enjoy having ..."

"I would prefer if..."

"I would appreciate it if..."

"I like it when you ..."

"Could you please ..."

"I need your help in ..."

"I'm hoping you'll..."

"Would you join me in ..."

"Could you get me ..."

"It would really be helpful if..."

Use feeling words more often than thinking words:

"I feel as if we ..." rather than "I think we ..."

The world is full of lonely people who won most of the arguments but lost the war—they were the dominating communication partner but ended up losing their relationship.

Make requests; don't issue orders:

"Could you ..."

"Would you ..."

"Will you ..."

"My request is that you ..."

Often, a brief statement of empathy before making a request helps soften any assertion you might make. For example:

"I need to request something of you ..."

"I can see you've been working hard ..."

"I know you wanted to relax today..."

"There's something I need to ask you ..."

"I need your attention for three minutes ..."

"Could I steal you away for a moment?"

"Let's sit down for a moment..."

Here are some gestures and statements to avoid because they'll reduce your chances of being self-confident. For example:

• Any of the unassertive phrases such as, "Let me repeat myself"

• Blaming language, such as, "It's your fault that..." or judgmental language, such as, "I think it was a bad idea for you to ..."

• Demanding language, such as, "Pay attention ..."

• Accusatory language, such as, "What's going on here ..."

• Abrasive language, such as, "Look, I only have a minute ..."

• Domineering language, such as, "I already told you ..."

Also, when asking a question, avoid language in which you apologize, such as, "I'm sorry to bother you with this, but . . . ," or ask for permission, such as, "May I ask you a quick question?" People often believe they are softening their request, but it makes a person sound unsure or timid.

As you engage in give-and-take dialog, depending on the situation and where the conversation is heading, use one or more of the following modes of conversation:

• Support the others' viewpoint, with phrases such as, "I think I understand where you're coming from..."

• Acknowledge the other person's non-vocal response by saying, "I know what I'm saying may come as a surprise..."

• Allow for other possibilities, such as, "I know you may see this differently..."

• Offer periodic praise, such as, "You've been good about this, bear with me for one more minute ...

• Offer links between points, such as, "So you see, adding A to B, I figure ..."

Obviously, I can't give you the vocal nuances that would make each of these phrases work as intended. Even if you used any one of them magnificently, that would not guarantee success. Still, using this kind of language in an engaging interpersonal manner will help enormously in many situations.

Because being self-confident with a spouse or significant other is special, you may have to extend yourself even further than what I've just covered. I mean, hey, you're going to have endless conversations that involve some form of give-and-take. So, periodically try some approaches that help grease the skids.

Admit When You're Wrong

I don't know anyone who really likes to do this, but doing it on occasion creates an environment in which you keep your credibility at a nice, high level. If you've ever known anyone who always insists they're right, you know how infuriating it is when such a person approaches you with yet another issue, especially when their position is once again questionable.

By freely acknowledging your own fallibility, you project yourself as a more balanced, rational, reasonable person.

Everyone is fallible—that is, subject to goofing, making errors, or in general being wrong about something.

Who would be more influential with you: Someone who always maintains his correctness, or someone who asserts himself for what he wants, but acknowledges he might make mistakes along the way?

Keep it Light

Sometimes, when making a request of a stern nature, your body language, posture, and demeanor don't need to be stern. If you play the heavy all the time, especially when making requests of others who regularly comply with your requests, they will regard being around you as burdensome.

Your Children

What's the matter with kids today? Probably nothing more than what was the matter with kids of the previous generation.

I'm not a child psychologist, and chances are you aren't either. Neither of us needs to be one, however, when it comes to being self-confident with our children. If you treat your children as full-fledged human beings from the time they are small, they'll respond to you in ways only previously imagined.

You can be much more self-confident when you say some things with a smile or a twinkle in your eye, because the other party finds your approach so much more palatable.

Lording over someone, even if that someone happens to be your child, is rarely as effective as being self-confident with them in the short run, and it never is in the long run. You can, however, employ all of the ideas about self-esteem that you learn in this book with your children.

Treating your children like full-fledged human beings doesn't mean treating them like adults. They are, however, individuals with their own sets of likes and dislikes, perceptions, and notions about the world.

When you speak to another person in your office or around town, do you use language that is similar to the following:

• "Because I know what's best for you ..."

• "Because I said so ..."

• "I don't want to say it again ..."

• "If I have to ask you one more time…"

• "If I have to tell you one more time …"

• "Never mind what I do …"

Hopefully, the answer to my question above is that you never use such language with other adults. Why? It simply wouldn't work. They'd look at you, roll their eyes, and tell you to get off it, and that's the most polite language they might use.

Why, pray tell, would you believe that using such language would be effective with your children? Is it because you:

• Heard it from your own parents?

• Saw it on television?

• Believe your children are unintelligent?

• Heard something somewhere about something called tough love and think you're dispensing it?

• Don't know how else to make a request?

Your assignment is to forever banish unassertive communication patterns with your children to the far corner of the universe.

The statements above use unassertive language and demotivate people. They do not prompt action, inspire others, or leave the other party feeling good about the interaction.

Don't let any minor or temporary "success" you think you achieve by using these statements cloud your view. You might be winning battles, but you'll be losing the war. Anyone who is confronted with such language may concede and bow to your demands, but they do so begrudgingly. The last thing you need to create is a rebel in your own family. You have enough problems already!

Okay, you ask, how do I get little Justin or Kristen to respond to my requests?

Here, in order and without adornment, is composite advice from leading child psychologists and authors on what your child wants and needs. Receiving these items on a regular basis will make your child more than willing to capitulate to most of your requests most of the time —by golly, the first time you ask!

• Love your children and demonstrate it. Love may not conquer all, but it conquers a lot.

Do you go out of your way to do things for the people you love? When you love your children, they tend to love you back and honor much more of what you request.

• Spend some time with your children each day. I don't care how hectic it gets at work, what your responsibilities are, or what your life is like in general.

A lot of rubbish has been written in the last two decades about the importance of spending "quality" time with your children. What exactly is the lack of quality time—junk time? Given the choice between spending an hour with you in less than the best circumstances and five minutes of "quality" time with you, I assure you most children will choose the hour. To them, quantity equals quality in many regards.

If you simply bop in and out of their rooms or in and out of their lives, however, the likelihood that you can be self-confident with them logically diminishes.

All the time you spend with your children can be quality time, even if you're only watching an inane television show. There are always things you can explain, conversation you can initiate during the commercials, and little tidbits of communication that go back and forth all show long.

• Constantly reinforce your children's behavior. Kids are approval and attention machines; at least they start out that way. Nine-tenths or more of what they do is either to get your approval or your attention. If you withhold your approval, they try even harder to get it. If you continue to withhold it, they give up in time and settle for getting your attention. The problem is that they may get your attention in ways you might not enjoy.

In terms of getting your children to listen and respond to you, this means that you can begin right now, today, even if your relationship with your children is somewhat strained. You can get them to listen and respond by "rewarding them" when they do things you want them to do.

Do you want your child to clean his room? The next time he cleans his room as well as every other time, offer responses such as the following:

"You've done a wonderful job here. Congratulations."

"Your room looks sparkling. You've done well."

"What a pleasure to walk into such a clean bedroom."

"I'm pleased to see the fine job you've done here."

"I love it when you clean your room."

"Excellent, excellent job!"

It's of no avail to comment three days later on the wonderful job your child did cleaning his room. Why? If your verbal, gestural, or material reward trails the performance over too great a time interval, the mental and emotional connection is lost.

In addition to your words, let your body language express your glee as well. Widen your eyes. Perk up. Smile. Convey your joy, pleasure, and rapture for your child's efforts in cleaning his room. You practically cannot overdo this. Even if you think it's not working, your support has a cumulative effect.

Each time you reward a child through gestures or verbal acknowledgment, you add to the probability that he'll clean his room again, more readily after your request. You may even reach the point where he cleans his room without you asking at all; the response he receives is so personally rewarding he cleans his room simply to receive it again.

Rewards

What about giving rewards such as money, a trip to the ice cream shop, or staying up late? These items can work. However, the situation is different for everyone. Dr. Aubrey Daniels, in his book Bringing out the Best in People, says that what motivates one person may not motivate another. You have to explore.

You have to specifically find out what works best for your child. However, this much is clear: Regardless of the reward you offer, it must closely follow the performance.

What kind of language can you use to reach the point when your child looks forward to cleaning his or her room or honoring any other request that you make? Try some of these on for size, noting that none of this is parent-to-child language; that is, "Because I told you to do it." Rather, this is person-to-person language. You're treating your child as a fully functioning human being, albeit a younger, smaller, less knowledgeable, or less-experienced version of an adult.

• "I'd like you to clean up your room now."

• "It's important that you finish your homework by seven. Please get started on it in the next couple of minutes."

• "It's okay if you don't want to finish all your vegetables, but I'd like you to eat at least half of them."

• "Would you prefer to take out the garbage or dry the dishes?"

• "You can stay out until 9:30 p.m., but no later. This is a school night, so I look forward to seeing you at 9:30, or before."

The Eldest Child

The eldest child in the family has different characteristics than those of succeeding children. For example, among many, the eldest child tends to be more adventurous. She may be inclined to travel more; live further from her original, nuclear home; and take more risks personally and socially.

In cases where the eldest child is put in charge of the other children, the child might have had a head start in becoming self-confident. If the eldest child is a female, she, in particular, may have had to practice parental, or more specifically, "mommy" skills at an early age.

As I've emphasized throughout, your ability to be self-confident is largely optional. Eldest child or not, you always have the choice to engage in self-confident behavior. Even if you are the youngest in your family, the opportunity to assert yourself is there for the taking.

Rejoice in the little ways that your children assert themselves. They'll need such skills when they get older.

Bossiness and Self-Esteem

Sometimes it's difficult for children to learn self-esteem. Often, self-esteem in making requests and standing or speaking up for yourself in a way that makes the other person feel good about the interaction slips into the realm of bossiness.

Children are perfect mirrors of our own behavior. All studies show that the habits you engage in are likely to be picked up by your children, whether it's smoking, swearing, driving too fast, or abusing your spouse.

If you boss your children around, not treating them as full-fledged human beings but as your property or chattel, don't be surprised to find them bossing around their siblings or other children. After all, they imitate you, and they're probably doing a good job of it.

Lucy in the "Peanuts" comic strip is the epitome of the bossy personality. Lucy calls people names. She doesn't make requests; she issues demands. There are times when the other kids barely tolerate her. She is the one who causes Charlie Brown to say, "Good grief!" more often than anyone else. If you want your kids to act like Lucy, keep yelling at them, bossing them around, and haranguing them for what they did not accomplish.

So…

- To be effective with members of your immediate family, you need to connect with them so that they feel you're on their side.

- Because being self-confident with a spouse or significant other is special, you may have to extend yourself even further.

- "Communication problems" is most frequently cited by survey respondents as the top reason for divorces in America.

- Rejoice in the little ways that your children assert themselves. They'll need such skills when they get older.

- Children are perfect mirrors of our own behavior.

Your Parents and Other Relatives

Are you among the many people who have longstanding miscommunications with your relatives? By relatives I mean parents, mothers-in-law, fathers-in-law, uncles, cousins, nieces, and nephews, whether they are of the first, second, or once-removed variety. Vast numbers of people have problems in this area. If they didn't, Hollywood movies and endless TV sitcoms wouldn't profit from milking "mother-in-law" scenarios and jokes decade after decade.

In this section, I'll take a look at your ability to be self-confident with different categories of relatives, including your parents, your spouse's parents, uncles and aunts, nieces and nephews, cousins, and other relations, both near and far.

Parents

If you've ever stayed at your parents' home after years of living on your own, undoubtedly you found yourself falling back into familiar communication patterns. Perhaps your parents have house rules that you don't fully agree with. Perhaps they criticize you or nag you, and you respond. Perhaps your communication pattern even reverts back to when you lived there as a child, a teenager, or young adult.

With all the exclamation in the world, you can say, "MOTHER!" or "FATHER!" and your mother or father will give you rapt attention. If your parents are like most parents, tell them that you really have to talk to them, and you've got their attention.

Nevertheless, for many people, being self-confident with their parents is among the easier tasks when it comes to self-esteem. Why? They cut you more slack. They give you more latitude.

The way to get your parents to listen and respond is much the same as you'd proceed with your spouse, children, or anyone else you're close to. You can go back and reapply what you've already learned to situations with your parents.

There are a few nuances to asserting yourself with your parents. If you can steer clear of some of these pitfalls, then you greatly enhance your ability to get your parents to listen and respond.

Speak to your parent adult-to-adult. Don't fall into any role you might have played when you were six, 11, or 19. If you revert back to childlike communication with your parents, chances are it will evoke responses from your parents similar to those of the past.

Be secure in your role as an adult, and your parent or parents will have no choice but to respond to you as an adult.

• Avoid being manipulated by guilt. You call your mother. She answers and says, "Oh, hi. I was so surprised. You hardly ever call anymore!" This is the part where you don't fall for it.

If your mother (or father, just as well) wants you to call more often, she needs to buy this book, practice self-confident behavior, and pay homage to the principle that rewarded behavior tends to be repeated. If she wants you to call more often, each time you call she should say something like:

"It's wonderful to hear from you."

"I'm so happy when you call."

"The sound of your voice is comforting to me."

81

"How are you doing; I've been thinking about you!"

If you're face-to-face with your parents and they attempt to make you feel guilty, don't respond to it. Suppose your father says, "Is it too much to ask you to blank blank blank." If you say yes, you contribute to a climate of potential hostility and hurt feelings. If you say no, you capitulate to his wishes and set yourself up for further manipulation and feelings of guilt another time. What would be a more appropriate response? How about:

"What's the real issue behind all this?"

• Don't allow your parents to offer prolonged criticism. Because they're your parents, they may feel entitled to criticize you, and some criticisms can actually be objective, valid, and even helpful.

It's much too easy to fly off the handle in the face of criticism from your parents, especially when you're an adult. "You never approved of anything that I..." Don't reciprocate with anger or criticize in return. Instead, assert yourself! The more balanced and even-toned you remain, the more your parents get the message that you're not willing to engage in the same old unproductive behavior patterns anymore.

Tired of being criticized by your parents? Try making a request about how you'd like to discuss the issue. Tell them how you'd like them to offer recommendations that they think might be helpful for you in the future.

In-Laws

You'd think the more you get to know your spouse's parents and vice versa, the less potential there is for any misunderstanding. But I have not encountered a study correlating the length of time you know your in-laws with your ability to communicate effectively with them. Indeed, some people naturally hit it off in a matter of seconds, while others don't seem to connect effectively, even after years of knowing one another.

The possible causes for the difficulty you may have communicating effectively and/or being self-confident with your in-laws are as numerous and diverse as personality characteristics among human beings. Here are a few of the possibilities. Perhaps your in-laws:

• Regard you as an outsider, someone who has invaded their nuclear family (even if their son or daughter is a full-fledged adult in society, left their household more than a decade ago, and chose a partner wisely).

• Are insecure about their relationship with their son or daughter and feel you may represent some type of threat to that relationship.

• Never warm up to anybody, and you just happened to many into their family.

• Have unrealistic expectations about the kind of partner their son or daughter would find in life, and try as you might, you'll never live up to those expectations.

• Can't concede that you had a life before you met their son or daughter and hence, regard you as something less than a fully functioning human being.

• Have always had trouble communicating with their son or daughter and now are extending that inability to include you.

• Subconsciously never wanted their child to many. After all, that's a signal that they're aging.

• Liked someone else their child dated before you and wanted that person to be part of their family. Thus, anyone who comes after, in their minds, will never completely live up to their expectations.

• Are prejudiced about your background, education, religion, social status, ethnic origin, or some other personal characteristic. There are Archie Bunkers in the world, even though, miraculously, their children sometimes grow up to be nice people.

• Connect you with someone else who made them feel uncomfortable, or they simply don't like your looks.

• Resent compromises their child has made to be in a marital relationship with you. For example, you may have ended up moving far from the in-laws' home, or you're in a profession that demands odd hours or prolonged travel.

• Feel they never see their child enough, and now they will see him or her even less with you in the picture.

• Feel their ability to communicate with their child was unique and special and that anyone else in the "channel" is a distracting or disruptive element.

• Have not had a happy marriage, and they project onto your marriage the same misery and misfortune. Thus, without knowing you or attempting to get to know you, they surmise that you will be the cause of such misery for their child.

• Vigorously disapprove of some aspect of your life; for example, you have been married before, have children, smoke, drink, have a large dog, or drive a pickup truck, and they have let this single factor cloud their perception of you.

You can see from this extensive list above—and it could have been much longer—that many of the reasons why you may have communication and/or self-esteem problems with your in-laws have little to do with you.

Of course, there are things you could be doing to create the difficult situation—perhaps you expect them to be more like your parents, or blame them for difficulties their child has, and so on. Getting along is a two-way street!

In their book How to Keep People From Pushing Your Buttons, Dr. Albert Ellis and Dr. Arthur Lang note that the first step in not letting others upset you is to accept the fact that they can behave like "real creeps." This statement doesn't mean that they actually are creeps, but rather that they can behave that way. Moreover, there's nothing particularly wrong in feeling nervous, angry, concerned, guilty, upset, flustered, embarrassed, grief-stricken, displeased, or edgy on occasion, even in the proximity of your in-laws.

The key, say Drs. Ellis and Lang, is to realize that other people don't really control these emotions within us. We're in charge of the emotional control room of our lives, and we need to remember that. "When we worry too much about what others think of us or about getting respect, failing, or making fools of ourselves," say the authors, "we forget we're really the ones in charge of ourselves."

Let's look at a variety of encounters you may have with your in-laws, keeping an eye on how you can assert yourself when you need to and still have a life and a wife or husband.

First, I need to lay down a couple of ground rules. You might want to examine this list closely because these are non-negotiable:

1. You don't have to earn the right to be your spouse's husband or wife. You already did on the day you married.

2. You're going to have to be forgiving and forgiving and forgiving. As the late Dr. Norman Cousins once said, "Life is an adventure in forgiveness."

3. Relax. If you are calm and relaxed, you'll be perceived as being more emotionally intelligent, regardless of what else you do. In addition, if you intend to be married for a long time, you'll need this capability.

4. Give up the notion of trying to become what you think your in-laws want you to be.

Okay, now that you've fully absorbed these ground rules, here are some scenarios in which you can be self-confident with your spouse's parents, and still live to eat at their dinner table another day.

The Polite Decline

You'll undoubtedly be asked to do many things, such as have another helping of some food you cannot stand, spend another two hours with "Dad" tinkering with his car in the garage, or stay far longer at a family function than you can possibly stand.

Assuming that you've talked with your spouse in advance about your parameters for the endurance tests posed by your in-laws, offer a brief apology and excuse yourself. For example:

"It's been great, but it's getting kind of late."

"I'm sorry, I didn't realize the day was passing so quickly."

"As much as I'd like to, I simply couldn't force down even another bite."

"Thanks, I'll take a raincheck on that one."

Don't start apologizing left and right for things over which you are not sorry, or over choices you've made about your time or level of participation. Do not compromise yourself. Remember the essence of self-esteem:

• Conveying appropriate self-interest

• Maintaining integrity

• Upholding your rights as a person

You Can Leave Me Out of This One

Suppose you're drawn into an argument between your spouse and his or her parents or into an argument between the parents themselves. If you don't choose to be part of the encounter, you have a variety of options for bowing out gracefully:

• "I don't have a well-developed opinion in this area and, so, won't offer one."

• (Said while smiling) "Sony folks, I'm just not going to be drawn into this."

• "In all honesty, I don't see a part for myself in this particular discussion."

• "I'm going to bow out." (Then physically retreat from the scene by stepping out or simply walking away.)

• "I'm positive that I can't be helpful here."

• "I wish I had something worthwhile to contribute here, but I don't."

These kinds of statements enable you to withdraw from an argument probably as gracefully as can be done.

Don't Tread on My Spouse

Suppose you encounter a situation where one or both of your in-laws dump on your spouse. Perhaps they tell you anecdotes about what your spouse did when he or she was younger.

Perhaps they reveal some "deep, dark secrets" they feel you ought to know. If this is within earshot of your spouse and you want to have a long, happy marriage, you probably need to quash this mode of communication as quickly and courteously as possible.

If insights about your spouse are offered outside of his or her earshot, you need to quash this as soon as possible, no matter how juicy or enticing the anecdote is. Why? Turn the tables. Suppose your parents said the same to your spouse when you were not present. How would you feel if you found out later?

Parents and relatives sometimes feel they have the right to dispense such information because, after all, they're talking about their daughter, son, brother, or their sister. They feel that they know this person best and have observations that are long-term and seemingly helpful. Don't fall prey to this maneuver.

You may ask one of your in-laws for help in a particular area in relation to dealing with your spouse, but a major issue arises when they open up the broadcast channel and dispense whatever information they want to about your spouse and you willingly listen.

Here are a variety of potential responses:

• Ask, "Why are you telling me this?" (Wait for their response.) If the response is that your in-law thinks it will help you in your relationship, tell them something along the lines of "I'm already aware of this," "I prefer to find these things out for myself," or "I appreciate your concern but I prefer not to hear this."

• Change the subject. If this works, fine; if it doesn't, change the subject again. If your in-law still doesn't allow you to do this, try excusing yourself and leaving, using the restroom, or going for a walk.

Here, actions indeed speak louder than words. You send a clear message to your in-laws that this is not the kind of conversation in which you intend to engage. If they don't understand this time, they will the next time you leave.

Are You Talking to Me?

Suppose your in-laws have a nickname or pet name for you of which you don't approve. Or, suppose they label you in some way behind your back that is less than flattering. In the former case, simply saying, "I prefer to be called Bob" should be sufficient. If it's not, try suggesting, "Please, call me_____."

If you know your in-laws call you something behind your back or refer to you in some derogatory manner, going out of your way to convince them that you're just the opposite won't work. You'll then mute your own personality and capitulate to their erroneous notions.

As for labels your in-laws may use to refer to you (behind your back or told to you by your spouse), the best advice in terms of standing up for yourself is to ignore it. Such labels might include egghead, dizzy, fashionable, homeboy, and so on.

You need to be yourself, with them and away from them. Hopefully, their labels will drop off as they learn more about you, but if they don't, you're better off ignoring the issue. If you challenge or question the image your in-laws have of you, you may never live it down.

Leave Me Out of This

I wouldn't wish this on you, but suppose one or both of your in-laws are non-stop complainers. Almost every time you encounter them, they yap about the government, economy, media, neighbors, or something else. Suppose they feel the need to place blame on everything large and small for the things that are not going right with the world or their lives.

Misery may or may not like company. The psychic toll that results from complaining and blaming behavior is not worth any fleeting feelings of camaraderie that might surface in your relationship with your in-laws if you decide to join in.

Some people constantly fuel their conversational fires by complaining and blaming. For some, this has become such an ingrained part of their daily routine that they no longer recognize how much of their conversation and thoughts are consumed by negative thoughts. If you start playing their game, hoping to win them over, yours will be a shallow victory.

Social Psychology 101 tells us that if parties A and B have a common enemy C, parties A and B are united. However, that unity lasts only as long as C is present. Suppose that A is your in-laws, B is you, and C is every little thing they like to complain about, or someone in particular. Remove C, and A and B may find themselves at war with each other. Otherwise, they need D to come along, so they can renew their common dislike of a single target. This approach to forming a relationship does not create much of a union.

Realistically, you're not going to change your in-laws. It took them 60 years to become who they are, and they're perfect at it. They're not going to change in 60 minutes, 60 hours, or 60 days, even if you have a Ph.D. in psychology. You can politely decline to participate in their complaining and blaming routine by pointing out something to the contrary, as you'll see in the following examples:

• They say, "The government is always trying to squeeze every nickel out of us." You say, "It seems that way sometimes; but the government has sponsored some good programs such as the XYZ."

• They say, "TV is worse than a vast wasteland; it's a sludge pile of porn, violence, and inane sitcoms." You say, "Much of TV is; but, with all the channels we can receive today, there are some good programs on. Do you ever watch The Learning Channel, The Discovery Channel, or the Public Education Network?"

• They say, "I don't think that doctors have any clue about what I'm experiencing. With all the money they're making you'd think they'd have some answers." You say, "It's hard for anyone, no matter how educated, experienced, or equipped, to fully understand somebody else's health problem. There are things we can do for ourselves, such as_____."

By now, you set the drift; no matter what their lament is, you can offer another way to look at the situation. The larger issue is, why bother offering them a counterpoint? Your argument may help, but then again, it may not. If you offer a counterpoint, it might start an argument. If you don't offer a counterpoint, then politely try to hang in there or change the subject. The choice is yours. At no time, however, should you become a party to their gripe-and-blame game.

Could You Say That Another Way?

Suppose one of your in-laws is notorious for his or her use of profanity. Every other word or sentence offends you. You're not sure if they use profanity for shock effect or if they simply talk this way to everyone. The point is, you don't like it.

It's hard to think of something to say to lessen this person's use of profane language. No matter what you say, you'll sound like a prude, a persnickety person, or a holier-than-thou type. One possible strategy, and this is certainly not for everyone, is to let the other party know you're also fully capable of using such language although you normally choose not to.

If you're not comfortable with the idea of letting out a string of four-letter words following profanity from one of your in-laws (or anyone), and chances are you're not comfortable with this approach, try excusing yourself from any conversation where you're subjected to language you prefer not to hear. You can always go to the bathroom, the front porch, the backyard, the car, or take a walk around the block.

Previously, you learned that rewarded behavior tends to be repeated. Likewise, you can help extinguish another person's behavior by saying something like, "That kind of language makes me uncomfortable." Or you can withdraw. If mother-in-law X swears profusely in your presence and so you disappear, mother-in-law X may realize that to continue talking to you, she needs to clean up her act. She may not get your message, though. Either way, you won't be subjected to such language.

Getting Anyone Else You're Close to to Listen and Respond

With anyone else with whom you are close, you want to avoid old, unproductive communication patterns, listen carefully to what's being said, and use self-confident language when you want or need to speak or stand up for yourself.

Remember, the longer you are with anyone, the more easily you fall into communication routines. Therefore, it becomes more important to vary the structure of your sentences as well as the substance of your communication. Disarm your listeners on occasion by using bright, bold, colorful language that moves otherwise routine discussions to a new level.

For variety if nothing else, change your sentence patterns constantly. Instead of saying to someone, "I think I can help you here," try, "I see myself striding side-by-side with you as we take control of the situation and devise a system to make things stay in place."

Also, instead of saying, "I've heard what you said, and I'll get back to you," try something like, "What you've said is provocative and certainly merits considerable thought. I'm going to give your words serious attention and offer my plan as to where we can go from here. I appreciate how you've gotten the ball rolling and promise you won't be pushing it alone."

Too exuberant, you say? Disarming? Your communication partner will hardly believe it's you? Fine. That means that your words are likely to be all that more effective!

So...

- The trouble you have with your spouse's parents may have nothing to do with you and everything to do with them. Conversely, check your own behavior and attitudes toward them— maybe you're the source of the problem.

- You don't have to silently endure behavior from your spouse's parents that you wouldn't tolerate from others.

- All of your relatives deserve respect and understanding. In turn, so do you.

- Sometimes the best way to get your message across is simply to withdraw from a situation and leave the room.

- It's a big and often lonely world, and your relatives can help make it a more hospitable place.

6. Career and Self-Esteem

Now we come to that arena in which being self-confident can make the difference between a career that continues to progress at a healthy pace and one that is stifled. Being self-confident in the workplace, that modern-day jungle, is a prerequisite to higher pay, respect, and the corner office. If you doubt it, think about the people with whom you work who are not self-confident. Chances are they're the wimps. They do a good job, perhaps earn a decent wage, but they get passed over time and time again.

In terms of practicing self-esteem skills, the workplace is a special arena. Never mind all that stuff you've seen on inane television shows and movies where executives spar with each other in grandiose ways. There's enough real-life drama that you don't have to draw upon the false images the media conveys.

In this chapter, I'll explore the self-esteem issues that could make a difference in your job.

How, you ask, can self-esteem be a substitute for accomplishment, competence, and effort? Study after study shows that if you and a co-worker have similar education, training, and experience, and all other things about you are equal, the one who is effectively self-confident will predictably rise faster in his or her career.

Suppose two managers are alike in every respect—they have the same background, education, training, aptitude, skills, and so on. You know what this is leading to. One has no problem being professionally self-confident in the following areas:

• Airing his views

• Speaking up for himself

• Defending his turf

• Persuading others

• Speaking up at company meetings

• Making his ideas known

Given that you are a competent employee who dutifully executes the requirements of the job, the nature of your interpersonal communications at work—how self-confident you are—largely defines your progress.

The other manager is marginally effective in these areas. Who is more likely to rise faster and go further in his career? Okay, you say, this is a no-brainer. Anyone will say the first manager.

Now let's complicate the issue a bit. Suppose that two managers are alike in most respects, but the first is not quite as sharp, and doesn't quite have some of the technical knowledge possessed by the second manager, but is very good at expressing himself.

The second manager is very conscientious. He is a planner. Generally, he executes his tasks with precision. When it comes to expressing himself, however, there are some gaps in his ability. Sometimes he rambles on. Sometimes he's not forthcoming with his views when the situation calls for it. Sometimes, to know what he's thinking you practically have to pry it out of him. Nevertheless, he does a consistently good job and unquestionably is an asset to the organization.

Now, who's likely to rise faster and further in his career? The answer isn't so easy this time, is it? The odds remain that the first manager will rise faster even if he is lacking in some categories as compared to the second manager. Why? He has the ability to assert himself.

Before you start thinking, okay, well, the first manager has the gift of gab, he's a schmoozer—he talks his way up the chain—think again. The professional who is able to assert himself as necessary enjoys significant advantages over his otherwise more talented counterparts who are unassertive. For example, the self-confident professional can do the following:

• Adroitly express himself to others.

• Identify obstacles, hazards, and pitfalls of proceeding with a given plan.

• Better guard against requests of his time when he already is stretched to the max.

• Be more persuasive when influencing others to attain a desirable performance level.

• Establish alliances that can aid him in accomplishing his goals and the goals of others.

What might befall the more technically competent manager who is not as good at asserting himself? The following are all possibilities, although it's not likely that any one manager would be confronted by all of them:

• He ends up taking on more work than he can comfortably handle because he lacks the ability to indicate to others when he's overloaded.

• He may have trouble expressing frustrations over daily occurrences, how a project is going, and so on.

• He may not be as effective in supervising others. He may allow performance levels to slide because he is uneasy when it comes to verbally appraising others' efforts.

Until we can read each other's minds, the otherwise talented but unassertive manager is more likely to be stuck in terms of his overall career progress. He's more likely to stay at the same level longer than his more self-confident counterparts. And, sadly, he's more likely to be overlooked for raises and promotions.

If you doubt that any of this is true and you work in a large office with lots of other career professionals, make a few observations. On a scale of one to ten (with "one" being highly unassertive, and "ten" being highly self-confident) quickly and mentally rate who's in the larger or corner offices within your organization.

If there's only one corner office, who has it? If there are two, three, or four, who's occupying them? Chances are, you'll find self-confident types occupying this prime real estate.

To be sure, there are absolutely brilliant, talented, highly accomplished, non-self-confident career professionals. Someone like that may be seated in your chair right now. However, if you're not able to convey a sense of importance and even enthusiasm about your accomplishments —not able to "toot your own horn," even though what you've done may be a matter of record —hardly anyone will know what you've done.

Not even your own boss is likely to grasp the magnitude of your achievement. How could this be? You were asked to do xyz and you did xyz. Doesn't the performance speak for itself? Many times it does. Just as often, probably, the performance does not speak for itself. Perhaps:

• Others take it for granted.

• Others discount in their minds what you've done.

• Others don't recognize the true significance of your deed.

Let's face it, sometimes you may not even understand the value of what you've accomplished, and, if that's combined with an inability to assert yourself, you might as well be working in the basement of the building.

The dedicated, hardworking professional in the typical office who consistently does the job day in and day out but otherwise is unassertive, unfortunately gets passed over when it comes to the goodies and the kudos of work and of life. Here's an exercise to show you how this happens.

Draw up a list of the people in your office. Now go back to the list and put a star next to everyone who got a raise, got a promotion, got recognized, or was rewarded in some way recently such that others in the office including yourself have knowledge of it. For example:

Bill Williamson

Ahmad Maresh

Courtney Adams

Chris Colie

Roxanne Havers

Art Conners

Angela Freeman

Zack Debagan

Katharine Ayers

After you've finished placing stars by the appropriate individuals' names, review the list again. This time put an "A" at the end of the names of all individuals who on a purely personal and subjective scale you deem as being self-confident:

Bill Williamson A

Ahmad Maresh A

Courtnev Adams

Chris Colie A

Roxanne Havers

Angela Freeman

Art Conners

Zack Debagan

Katharine Avers

When you're through, look back at your list. What do you notice? Do most of the people with a star at the beginning of their name have an "A" at the end of their name? Is there one with simply a star or simply an A and not both? If there are, I'll bet the number is small.

The conclusion? Raises and self-esteem appear to have some significant correlation.

Getting Pay Raises

Given that you're doing a good job, being self-confident is probably the most important attribute you can have for getting pay raises.

What most people asking for a raise don't understand is that the cost of replacing them can be inordinate. Depending on what you do and how well you do it, your organization may well prefer paying you 5,10, or 15 percent more than you're currently making to having to place an ad, interview more people, bring somebody on board, get them up to speed, and see if they can actually do the job. The smaller the company, the more costly it becomes to replace good staff.

By now, you're probably drooling with anticipation. What exactly do you have to do to get a raise? What are the words, what are the gestures, how does the whole thing work? Actually, it's not complicated at all.

1. Determine in advance how much you want. This has to be in line with other factors, such as the pay range for your position and the budget allocated to your department. If you can't find these things out, try to determine what a reasonable percentage increase

would be. For example, have others in your firm received 8 percent raises? Or is 4 percent a more predictable figure?

2. Ask your boss for an appointment, or if that's too formal for your setting, at least reserve some time.

Perhaps you can take him or her to lunch. In any case, you want it to be known in advance that you have something important to discuss. Don't go into detail about why you want to meet—telling your boss you want to meet to discuss a raise would give him time to prepare his response.

3. Once you're face to face and ready to talk, make sure that both of you are seated. If you're standing, it's too easy for the conversation to be curtailed. The boss might be called away, or you may feel uncomfortable standing your ground for so long. Besides, you'll get more time with the boss if you're seated.

4. Cut right to the chase. By now, your boss knows there's something important on your mind. Let it out.

5. Use the classic irrefutable arguments: You've been doing very good work, you're requiring less

supervision, you're anticipating challenges to be better prepared for them, you're helping others on the team, you're going the extra mile, you're becoming more valuable to the organization, and so on. If it helps, bring up the parity issues. Other people with your experience, your education, or your age in similar positions in other organizations are earning x amount, and so forth.

Your boss may pooh-pooh your arguments in person; nevertheless, your points will register. If you can, come equipped with specific facts—preferably on paper—to back up these assertions. Instead of just saying you require less supervision, show evidence of a project that you handled solo.

6. If you can get approval at this one meeting, wow, you're a winner! It's more likely that your boss will ask for a follow-up meeting. Agree to it.

7. In the interim, continue to work hard, but don't bring up this issue.

8. When it's time to meet again on this issue, have some new points ready to add on top of the old ones. For example, just last week you were able to

accomplish xyz. Also, you took it upon yourself to straighten up the abc project, and you made a few extra calls to make sure that ghi. Emphasize all the little things you do that nobody tends to notice in addition to those things you do that are more apparent and visible.

9. If you encounter additional resistance, move to, "Okay then, by when?" Get your boss to commit. If she says "next quarter," "by next June," or by next anything, you've done well. Remember, in some cases, your boss truly is restricted as to what she can offer. Her budget may be fixed for the coming period.

However, there is always some financial slack in an organization when it conies to rewarding and retaining superior performance. You have only to find out what the CEO of your organization is making, including bonuses, and it will be abundantly clear that your organization can find the extra couple dollars per hour or thousands per year you're seeking.

10. Everything you've learned throughout this book about being self-confident comes into play when seeking a raise. You need to be a good listener. You need to give the other person a chance to respond.

You need to look her directly in the eye. You want to be professionally self-confident but not overbearing or cantankerous. You want to end the conversation on a cheerful note and march proudly back out the door.

Overstating your case is an indication to others that you're grappling with some other issue internally.

If someone is constantly complaining, say about the weather, the reality is he probably isn't so concerned with the weather as something else.

When you assert yourself, make sure that the time, place, and person are appropriate. It doesn't matter how self-confident you are if you ask someone to do something that he:

1. Can't understand in 100 years of explanation

2. Has no capacity or authority for undertaking

3. Might be able to accomplish but doesn't know where to begin

Offer your points in sequence based on chronology, order of importance, or other useful criterion. Some communication experts tell you to present your best point first, and your other points in descending order of importance.

Other communication experts suggest that you present your points in ascending order; that is, start with the least important ones and work up to the most important one. In this manner, the last point that you make is your best and most important and the one most likely to be remembered by your audience.

In my opinion it doesn't matter in what order you proceed—ascending, descending, or even offering your best point in the middle. More important is that you did a good job to begin with, you prepped your boss so that he or she knew that you were coming in to talk about something important, you reviewed the tips on self-esteem throughout this book, and you were your best self when you finally sat down and got around to talking about your value to the organization.

7. Advanced Self-Confidence Tips

This chapter expands upon what you learned in the previous chapters and gives you a framework for being more self-confident in every aspect of your life.

Too many people erroneously believe they have to be some type of exalted being to be self-confident because, after all, self-confident people never blow their tops. Au contraire! Anybody can get angry, even the most highly self-confident, self-confident people. However, the self-confident, self-confident person expresses his anger in a constructive manner as opposed to a destructive way (such as by shouting, threatening, insulting, or otherwise abusing others).

A paragon is a model of perfection or excellence—having no equal. Hence, no one is a paragon of self-confidence or self-esteem.

Likewise, the self-confident, self-confident person handles other challenges in a similar manner. More specifically, they:

- Identify what's needed.

- Express how they feel.

- Indicate what needs to be done.

- Refer to the bigger picture.

- Elicit agreement or cooperation.

- Close the discussion cordially.

There are people, and you may know some, who are self-confident most of the time. Sure, they face challenges that stymie them, and, like anybody, they can "lose it" on occasion. Generally, though, they approach each day and most situations with relative grace and ease. You can almost feel the calmness disseminating from the center of their being.

Paradoxically, self-confident people don't strive to be self-confident. It's almost as if they just allow themselves to "be." They seem to tap into internal resources that have, perhaps, been there all along, or—and this is exciting-are within each of us.

Self-confident people let vital qualities rise to the surface. They're not at war with themselves. Think of it—how would it feel if you were so self-assured that no one could shake your view of yourself?

Certainly, self-confident people have doubts about themselves, their work, and their lives in general. However, rather than try to force themselves to think and see everything as positive, they allow their doubts to be part of the total mix of their experiences. They don't allow their doubts to rule them. They maintain a level of honesty with themselves that draws on all of what they think and feel, sorts it out, and almost automatically redirects them toward the most appropriate thinking, behavior, and action.

A successful high school basketball coach was once asked by one of his mentors to join the college ranks as an assistant coach. This would mean an increase in salary and, perhaps, a chance to work as a head coach of a college team someday. The high school coach thought about it and said, "I'm flattered, but I have to decline. I know what I am; I'm a high school coach."

Did he show a lack of ambition, or was he simply being true to himself?

Optimism doesn't necessarily equate with high self-confidence. You can be pessimistic but self-confident. But if you are naturally optimistic, your ability to develop or maintain self-confidence is probably enhanced. If not, you still have a variety of everyday situations where you can "flex" your self-confidence muscle. Let's look at some of these situations, starting with self-confidence at work.

Self-Confidence at Work

Of all the people who will accompany you through each job, no boss, coworker, peer, spouse, parent, relative, or friend will be with you every step of your career journey; you're it! Similarly, you're the only one who can significantly increase the self-confidence you experience and convey to others. Once you accept that, you're practically halfway there. The six factors that follow, in combination with what you've learned in the previous chapters, will take you the rest of the way.

1. Work with a Coach

A career coach is not another term for mentor. This is a person you pay to help you.

119

In a nutshell, a career coach can:

- Organizational changes within your company, especially if they have a direct impact on you

- Acquisitions or mergers

- Expansion into new markets

- Diversification into new products or services

- Increased competition to your firm from other firms trying to take over your market share

- Increased management or supervisory responsibility

- Increased leadership opportunities

- A recent or soon-to-be available promotion

- A new boss or a leadership shake-up above you

- Changes in your role or assignments within your company

- In-company competition and power plays, corporate intrigue, jockeying for position, or turf protection

- Blockades of your progress by internal feuds or informal political processes

- Increased media exposure or public-speaking requirements

- Increased production or sales quotas

- A new project you must lead or participate in developing

2. Work with an Employment Contract!

An employment contract is a document that spells out your relationship with your employer and your compensation, benefits, job responsibilities, length of employment, and special incentives. The concept of generating an employment contract has been around for at least three decades. Unfortunately, most career professionals have no idea what it is, how to draw one up, or how to ensure that they only work with a contract.

Why address the notion of an employment contract in the middle of a chapter on everyday self-confidence in a book about self-esteem? Having an employment contract is a great confidence booster. Essentially, it defines your working conditions for the length of a specified term. It establishes your compensation rate. It practically secures your employment.

The kicker is, the contract enhances your confidence while you're writing it and gives you practice in acting assertively, both when you first broach the subject with your prospective or current employer, and when you actually conduct the session to consummate the contract negotiation.

In all industries, the most valuable people work with a contract. This is true in Fortune 500 companies; Major League Baseball; the highest levels of government; philanthropic organizations; and chic, social, and charitable organizations. The top talent works with employment contracts. In fact, the inability of management and an agent, representing some top performer, to agree on contract terms is often front page news.

3. Become Indispensable on the Job

Distinguish yourself from the rest of the pack at work by becoming indispensable. Here's a summary of the many strategies you can employ to become the kind of employee your company can't live without:

- Take the job no one else wants.

- Go the extra mile.

- Work harder when the cat's away.

- Get credit for your group.

- Make your boss look good.

- Become a mentor (ad hoc advisor or counselor) to junior or new members of your company.

- Figure out what's needed, not what's expected.

4. Know Your Product or Service Line Cold

In state legislatures, the senator who knows the most about the specifics of the legislation that has passed, is pending, or is about to be signed has an advantage over his peers. The sales professional who knows his product or service line cold is more confident in front of prospective buyers and customers and with peers, bosses, and top company management. The health care professional who learns about the latest equipment, diagnostic procedures, and patient care techniques automatically becomes a more valuable and more confident employee.

When you know as much or more about your products and services than anyone in the organization:

- Your self-confidence automatically increases.

- Co-workers and staff members naturally turn to you.

- Bosses and those higher up consider you a valuable resource.

- You're more confident in front of clients, customers, constituents, and other business contacts.

- Your oral and written communication abilities naturally grow stronger.

You don't need to know everything. Rather, you want to identify the critical information that will keep you at the forefront of your profession. This requires far less time and energy than you would think. Watch one less television show per day, for example, and you will probably have more than enough time to do this.

5. *Increase Your Professionalism at Work*

Every organization has its weak points.

Every boss has his or her shortcomings.

Every job has its drudgery.

It would be easy for you to compose a list of all that's wrong at your place of work. Perhaps you can write an article about it, or even a full-length book! Rather than travel that road, increase your level of professionalism a notch or two.

Straighten up your desk and office. Rearrange the pictures, posters, and plaques on the wall. Acquire the support items that will make you more productive. Consolidate material in files, on shelves, and in supply cabinets. Consolidate reminder notes, pads, and slips of paper, so your office is no longer covered with them.

Beyond improving the overall organization and appearance of your office, how about creating a more professional you? Do you need to get your hair trimmed or have your fingernails manicured? Do you need to dry-clean some of your suits? What can you do to improve your overall appearance?

6. Act with Greater Decisiveness

Effective executives tend to make decisions more quickly, and they don't retreat from them. This doesn't mean that they're bold and impetuous, but rather, they have learned to trust their instincts. Instinctive decisions aren't made out of the blue, but are based on a complex set of decision-making guidelines that have been developing inside of you for years.

When your gut and your head come up with the same decision, it's a lock. That is, when your intuitive or internal feeling along with any rational decision-making process that you've undergone are in agreement, don't have any qualms regarding making the decision. When your gut and your head disagree, go with the gut.

Being self-confident doesn't automatically qualify you for the self-esteem hall of fame. A variety of situations, techniques, and approaches still require discussion, and we've got the whole rest of this book to do that.

So...

- You have what it takes to be more self-confident in your life.

- At work you can practice increasing your self-confidence a little bit at a time by volunteering to head up projects, pitching in when you weren't asked, relieving some of your boss's burden, reorganizing your office, and cultivating a more professional appearance.

- Away from work, look for opportunities to help others, smile more often, approach someone you're attracted to, and start up a conversation with someone you don't know.

- You know you have self-confidence when it comes to you automatically—you don't have to think about it or practice it.

8. Conclusion

The next time you're in a meeting or listening to someone and you're thinking to yourself, "Should I speak up here? Maybe it will be more trouble than it's worth," I suggest to you that that's probably a good time to assert yourself.

Yes, occasionally you will go overboard and say too much. There will also be times when in retrospect it would have been better if you had said nothing. This will happen. This is life. You'll learn from those encounters and get better at training yourself to know when it's time to speak up. Still, heed your internal voice. If you think you ought to say something, the chances are extremely good that yes, this is an instance in which it makes sense for you to speak up. Don't let the handful of times where you err block you from the multitude of other times in which asserting yourself appropriate.

Made in the USA
Middletown, DE
24 October 2018